Hi Art,
Enjoy Humboldt Wild!
love, Arleen

Black-tail bucks

Humboldt Wild

photography by Arleen Olson

Left: A ranch nestles in the rolling hills of southern Humboldt County beneath Bear Butte.

Above: Juvenile Red-tailed Hawk

Black Sand Beach, beginning just north of Shelter Cove, stretches for miles along the roadless Lost Coast. Telegraph Creek, in foreground, empties into the Pacific during winter months.

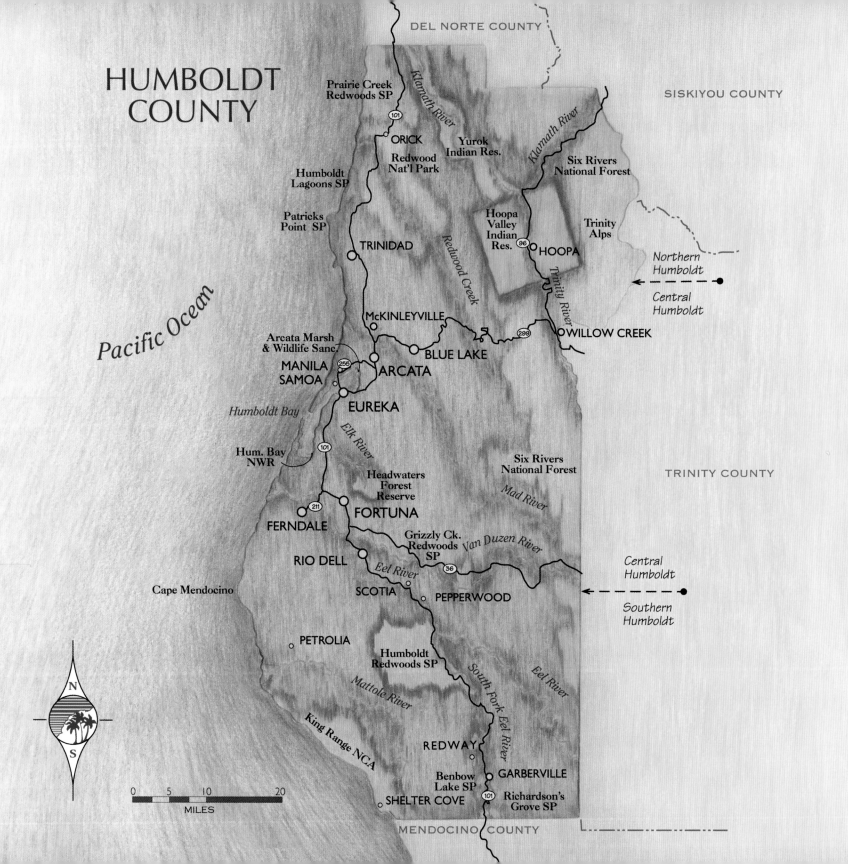

HUMBOLDT COUNTY

DEL NORTE COUNTY

SISKIYOU COUNTY

Pacific Ocean

Prairie Creek
Redwoods SP

Klamath River

101

ORICK

Yurok
Indian Res.

Redwood
Nat'l Park

Klamath River

Six Rivers
National Forest

Humboldt
Lagoons SP

Patricks
Point SP

Hoopa
Valley
Indian
Res.

Trinity
Alps

TRINIDAD

Redwood Creek

96

HOOPA

*Northern
Humboldt*

*Central
Humboldt*

McKINLEYVILLE

Trinity River

Arcata Marsh
& Wildlife Sanc.

BLUE LAKE

299

WILLOW CREEK

MANILA
SAMOA

255

ARCATA

Humboldt Bay

EUREKA

Hum. Bay
NWR

101

Elk River

Six Rivers
National Forest

TRINITY COUNTY

Headwaters
Forest
Reserve

Mad River

211

FORTUNA

FERNDALE

Grizzly Ck.
Redwoods
SP

Van Duzen River

RIO DELL

Eel River

36

*Central
Humboldt*

Cape Mendocino

SCOTIA

PEPPERWOOD

*Southern
Humboldt*

PETROLIA

Humboldt
Redwoods SP

Eel River

Mattole River

South Fork Eel River

King Range NCA

REDWAY

Benbow
Lake SP

GARBERVILLE

SHELTER COVE

101

Richardson's
Grove SP

MENDOCINO COUNTY

N
S

0 5 10 20
MILES

Contents

Top Left: Mariposa Tulip (*Liliaceae Calochortus*)
Bottom Left: An American Coot takes off on the duckweed-covered Arcata Marsh.
Top Right: Sea stacks from the coastal scenic route south of Trinidad
Bottom Right: Wild Things!
Next Page: Oregon oaks (*Quercus garryana*) silhouetted against a winter sunset

Marine influenced weather can create some dramatic skies.

Dedication

I dedicate this to my mother and father, Fran Bruning and Gustaf Olson who together infused me with positive thinking and a committed work ethic. As Mom would say, " If you can dream it, Do It!"

Acknowledgements

Many thanks to my intrepid pilots: Thomas Fisher, Andreas Pascal, Dan Greebe, and a special tribute to Birk Snow who died in a tragic airplane crash in Idaho. Birk was an avid defender of the environment and a humanitarian of the highest degree.

I would also like to thank my artist mentors, Nan Penner and Lauris Phillips, for their support and valuable feedback. Special thanks goes out to Jennifer Keegan (Jenny Big Help), without her help this book would never have been completed. And to Clyde Spears and Jay Peltz who are always there in an emergency.

I want to express my deep appreciation to those who helped me with this book: to Kathy Glass for her work on the captions, to Jerry Siever for the beautiful map of Humboldt County, and to Rixanne Wehren for the map graphics. I would like to thank photographer Richard Blair for his professional advice. I am especially indebted to Jeri Fergus for her help with design and layout, and to Joanne Bolton for her patience and assistance.

Thanks also to the knowledgeable professionals who helped identify plants and wildlife: to Bob Wick and Dave Fuller from BLM; to Denise Homer, Interpretive Naturalist for the City of Arcata; to Jim Wheeler, Park Ranger and Interpreter for Redwood National & State Parks; to Scott Adams, Outdoor Recreation Planner for the King Range; and to Dave Stockton, Executive Director of Humboldt Redwoods Interpretive Association.

Canada Geese with their goslings find a seasonal home in the Arcata Marsh.

Bear Grass (*Xerophyllum tenax*) in flower at King Range National Conservation Area; usually growing straight up, the flowers bloom in the second season after a burn, as this one did two years after the Honeydew fire.

Humboldt Wild

*O*ne of my fondest childhood memories is of visiting my great aunt in her big Victorian home. She would seat me in an over-stuffed chair surrounded by exotic plants and give me stacks of *National Geographic* magazines to look at to keep me out of trouble. It worked! There, I explored the beauty of the world and its diverse cultures, dreaming that some day I would see it all for myself.

Growing up in suburban New Jersey didn't offer me a chance to do this until after I graduated from Kean University. Then I took an anthropology course with the curator of the Museum of Natural History in New York and became inspired to work at an archeological site in Arkansas, where I eventually became the staff photographer for the Arkansas Archeological Survey. Through the AAS, I had the opportunity to explore that unique countryside and the people so foreign to me, from the deltas in the south to the beautiful Ozark Mountains to the north. I joined the local spelunking society and photographed and led expeditions in the amazing limestone caves there.

I still had a craving to experience the rest of the US, so I headed to San Francisco. Then, because I missed a rural atmosphere, I settled in Marin County. For many years I photographed some of the most beautiful homes in the world for the Marin County Board of Realtors and Marin Real Estate Magazine…until the county became too crowded and too unaffordable.

I found my piece of paradise 200 miles north in the mountains of Southern Humboldt County. I felt at home again. I worked for EPIC, the Environmental Protection Information Center, for almost five years, which gave me first hand knowledge of the destruction of this area's precious resources in the clear cutting of old-growth redwoods and the undermining of the health of the rivers and fish. In 1996 I opened a photography studio in Redway. This being such a small community, I diversified my work to

Moss on an oak tree plumps up when the fall rains come.

include fine art, portraiture, and commercial products. I photographed artwork, high school sports and graduations, Little League and youth soccer, and special occasions such as weddings, batmitsvahs, reunions, and baby showers…and much more! All this opened doors to parts of the county I'd never seen.

The more I explored, the more I realized what a truly amazing place Humboldt County is. *Humboldt Wild* is a chronicle of my explorations of these wild surroundings and the wild spirit of the people who inhabit Humboldt. Self-publishing this book was a monumental task that evolved over seven years. When organizing the chapters, I created the divisions of Southern, Central, and Northern Humboldt so that most of the residential areas lie in Central Humboldt, the hub of the county. The Special Events section is chronological and most of these events are fundraisers for local non-profit agencies.

I've seen the destruction of our forests & rivers, but fortunately nature constantly renews herself so we can still witness vast remaining wild places helped and protected by the efforts of many.

I hope that *Humboldt Wild* inspires others to appreciate and protect the incredible natural diversity that is Humboldt County.

In wildness is the preservation of the world.

Henry David Thoreau

Arleen Olson

The legendary Bigfoot is kept alive in chainsaw carvings and the occasional local report.

The fact that I can call Humboldt County my home is a source of great joy and pride to me. I think I share that love of place with many who live here, for if you enjoy the natural world, there is no better place for almost endless, delightful discovery. This county is diversity personified. From east to west, north to south, the mountains to the seashore, there's something beautiful around every corner. Though her bounty has nurtured human residents for thousands of years, the human footprint is moderate. No giant feats of human engineering dominate. Instead, here is nature in her myriad forms.

To us who live in Humboldt County, the concept of independence is very strong. The metropolitan areas are distant in both miles and atmosphere, and we like it that way. Here you might be lucky enough to wake up in a mountain home to see the valleys fill in with sea fog and the tops of the mountains floating above that white sea like islands in some mystical kingdom. It's not hard to see the beauty of this county if you just stop. And look. And listen. Nature here can be dramatic, it can be subtle. I doubt that I am the first to say that I have felt touched by the Divine when in the presence of some of the most magnificent trees on the planet, those massive redwoods of which we are so proud, or when on the powerful, primal Lost Coast.

I remember the day Arleen asked me to write something to be included in this book. It was a Sunday, at the end of February and I was visiting her at her home in the mountains east of Garberville. A storm was arriving preceded by strong winds, and the huge sky was filled with racing clouds. The light was incredible. On the way home, I mused on what makes Humboldt County special. Coming down the mountain, crossing from east to west, there was so much to capture the imagination—the rocky outcrops covered with lichen, the rolling hills

Lone fir tree silhouetted by the sunset

reminding me of my native Ireland, the oaks dripping with Usnea moss, and the South Fork of the Eel River winding its way through canyons of oak, fir, madrone, and what remains of the once giant redwood forest that covered this beautiful corner of California. And that was all in just a ten-mile drive!

The climate too, is a source of wonder to those who have come to realize its amazing diversity. On a typical summer day, residents who can't take the scorching inland sun can, in the space of a short drive or bike-ride westward, cool themselves by the magnificent Pacific. They might even pass their neighbors heading inland for the opposite reason! If you're lucky enough to live in Humboldt County, even the passage of the seasons is a cause for wonder and enjoyment. Don't be fooled by that old saying that there are only two seasons in California. In Humboldt County, at least, that just isn't so.

As you turn the pages in this beautiful book of photography, do so slowly. Take the time to immerse yourself in the atmosphere captured here so beautifully by Arleen Olson. Enjoy the journey. Welcome to *Humboldt Wild*.

Estelle Fennell
KMUD News Director from 1990-2007

Long-tubed Iris (*Iris tenuissima*) and Western Buttercups (*Ranunculus occidentalis*) brighten hillsides in spring

*I*t is always a pleasure to read a book that gives Humboldt County, and especially Southern Humboldt, the care and insight it deserves. Four generations of Stocktons have witnessed a wild and hostel land transformed through stages of exploration, resource extraction, boom industry, recession, depression, and post war boom to a still somewhat wild, somewhat tamed area of beauty that rivals, if not surpasses, that of the most beautiful places on earth.

Through the years there have been many historical books written about Humboldt County. A few have dealt with pictorial and natural aspects of the area while others have dealt with specific themes. Inevitable, the authors drift to the northern part of the county and leave Southern Humboldt a few photographs and some footnotes.

Arleen Olson, in her book *Humboldt Wild*, has made a drastic departure from this old formula. This book gives Humboldt County its due as a diverse, beautiful, scenic, and spiritual place that is time worn and yet timeless. It also covers the whole county with a large share of the features of Southern Humboldt included. Many citizens of this county are still close to the land and share a sense of place as well as a sense of connection with it, the unique ecologies, and the close-knit community. Connections exist in a many stranded tapestry that shows the individuality of the area as strongly as its cohesion.

There has always been something special about Southern Humboldt and it can be traced back to about fifty million years ago when a giant land plate split at Cape Mendocino. The northern part of this plate moved northeast while the southern portion moved somewhat east. Something here caused this giant landmass to split even though the coast was still under water. Geologists speculate this will happen again this time going inland from the coast all the way to Nevada. Recently the Mendocino triple junction has been moving north and is now in the area of the Devils Hole between Bull Creek

Trillium ovatum, also known as Wake Robin, is found on moist forest floors and along stream-banks in the redwoods. Appearing white at first, the bloom then turns pink.

and Honeydew. According to local legend, the Native Americans gave a wide birth to this place considering it an evil and threatening abode of bad spirits.

The "bad places" were more than compensated for by the bounty of food and materials for a high standard of living on a nearly year round basis. With an intensive management plan and constant implementation the Native Americans in the area enjoyed a comfortable and even wealthy existence unknown in most of North America. By our dietary and food standards today, the Native Americans, in comparison, had a vastly superior level of nutrition in their diet.

European settlement was not such a wonderful time and in the process there pioneers displaced the indigenous population and began a resource extraction that is still unprecedented in all civilizations at any time. Agriculture, timber, fishing, and movement of goods to markets occupied an ambitious population for a century and a half.

The extraction phase is dwindling down causing a lot of Humboldt County citizens to look around at where we have been, what we have become, and at those that have worked to preserve what resources are left. We have a deep and rich heritage and as readers turn the pages of *Humboldt Wild* surprises will be plentiful as the meanings and connections of what is here now and where it has come from give them a sense of perspective and a depth of genuine experience. *Humboldt Wild* is that same Humboldt County that lives on both the physical and spiritual plane simultaneously.

Dave Stockton
Executive Director
Humboldt Redwoods Interpretive Association

Above: "Corkscrew Tree" in Prairie Creek Redwoods State Park; it is unknown what causes this rare aberration in redwoods.

Right: Sentinels of time, the ancient Coast Redwoods (*Sequoia sempervirons*) are the world's tallest trees and among the longest lived, exceeding 360 feet and living up to 2000 years.

Humboldt Wild

Southern Humboldt

Humboldt Wild

Above: White-tailed Kite "kiting"

Right: Moonset at dawn over the King Range and Bear Butte

The east side of the King Range has the reputation as the wettest place in the state, with more than 120 inches of rainfall annually.

Geologists call this rock/soil type the "Yeager formation" with its fractured rock outcroppings. This was once the ocean bottom but tectonic plates moved the mountains upward.

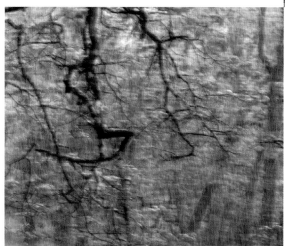

Left: Rain and branches in the wind—a common cameo of spring storms.

Above: A gnarled Buckeye tree grips its sheltered spot on the rocky hillside.

Humboldt Wild

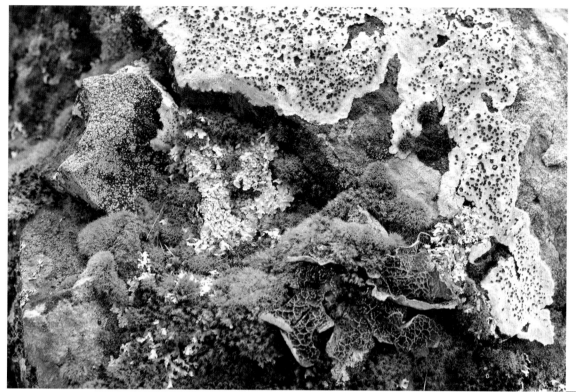

Above: The brown growth is liverwort; the green and pale growths are moss and lichens—evidence of a healthy ecosystem.

Right: Fruiting bodies of a Cup fungus

The ubiquitous wild lupine graces the oak forest landscape
and signals that spring is here!

Left: Tiny spring beauties: Elegant Cats Ear (*Calochortus elega*)

Middle: California Indian Pink (*Silene californica*)

Right: Smooth Yellow Violet (*Viola glabella*), common in moist forests and riparian areas

Left: A stormy view from Bell Springs Road near Harris
Right: The smoke from forest fires can create stunning sunsets.

Garberville perches above the winding South Fork Eel River along Highway 101.

Humboldt Wild

The South Fork of the Eel River winds its way through
Redwood forests.

Larabee Creek empties into the Eel River at Holmes, seen in this view of the confluence. Redwood trees edge lush farmland and the riverbanks.

Humboldt Wild

Above: Spawning males have bright red sides. The white fungus on the dorsal fins indicates that this salmon has almost completed his life cycle with this spawning effort.

Right: Salmon spawn in the South Fork Eel at Benbow State Recreation Area.

A Redwood twin looms above the Avenue of the Giants near Pepperwood. The 31-mile Avenue parallels Highway 101 and the Eel River south of Scotia as it passes through the Humboldt Redwoods State Park.

Above: "Old Home", near Weott, is a logging site dating from the early 1900s where laborers lived and worked in the redwood forest.

Right: This rare albino redwood is one of fewer than two-dozen that are known to exist. Lacking chlorophyll to convert sunlight into food, this "ghost redwood" must tap into the roots of a nearby tree for sustenance.

The remote Mattole River Valley lies to the west of the Eel River drainage.

Looking across the Mattole River estuary, the view northward is California's western- most point, Cape Mendocino. Shifting sands sometimes close off the river's mouth and create a lagoon during the summer season.

The Punta Gorda lighthouse, 3.2 miles south of the Mattole Beach, was built in 1912 and served until 1950. It was also known as the "loneliest lighthouse" because of its remoteness on the Lost Coast.

Above: Sea anemone in the inter-tidal zone

Right: Several species of crab inhabit area tide pools on the Humboldt coast.

Lightning on September 3, 2003 started this fire in the Honeydew area of the Mattole Valley. It burned more than 13,000 acres over two months. Though summer fires are a hazard to homesteads, they naturally clean out excess undergrowth in the Douglas-fir dominated forest ecosystem.

Humboldt Wild

The "Canoe Fire" burned 11,000 acres near Myers Flat, also in September of 2003, including parts of Humboldt Redwoods State Park. California Department of Forestry back-burned this forest to check its spread to the nearby town.

Wildfires can burn with varying intensity, in huge swaths or isolated patches, like this heart shape burned into the mountainside near Honeydew. The orange trees were killed by heat, not fire.

Humboldt Wild

Above: Fire has its positive aspects and plays a crucial role in the ecosystem. It helps release seeds for germination and creates open sky for young plants. These redwood sprouts are growing the year after fire passed through.

Right: In this post-fire landscape, fire "crowned" in the black areas and killed these trees.

 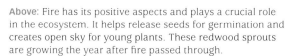

Left: Big Flat from King Peak. At 4,087 feet above the beach, King Peak is the highest point on the U.S. continental coastline (excluding Alaska). Only the hardy hike in to Big Flat Beach, about eight miles along Black Sand Beach from Shelter Cove.

Above: Skeletons of dry Manzanita scrape the sky near the top of King Peak.

Humboldt Wild

Lightning Trail leads to the top of King Peak. Administered by the BLM (Bureau of Land Management), King Range National Conservation Area became an addition to the U.S. Wilderness System in 2006. It covers 60,000 acres, with over 42,000 in wilderness areas, and extends along 35 miles of northern California coastline.

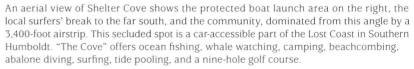

An aerial view of Shelter Cove shows the protected boat launch area on the right, the local surfers' break to the far south, and the community, dominated from this angle by a 3,400-foot airstrip. This secluded spot is a car-accessible part of the Lost Coast in Southern Humboldt. "The Cove" offers ocean fishing, whale watching, camping, beachcombing, abalone diving, surfing, tide pooling, and a nine-hole golf course.

Humboldt Wild

A tractor pulls a fishing boat from the water at Shelter Cove, the only launch area for about
40 miles in each direction on this rugged coastline.

Left: A memorial statue of mariner and entrepreneur Mario Machi stands watch in the fog at Mal Coombs Park in Shelter Cove.

Above: Built in 1868, the Cape Mendocino lighthouse originally occupied a site on California's westernmost headland near Petrolia. Earthquakes and high winds battered the structure and, like most lighthouses in the area, it was abandoned in the early 1950's due to new maritime technology. It was relocated to Mal Coombs Park in Shelter Cove in 1999.

Above: Brown Pelicans, once a threatened species, have made a comeback on the California coast. This popular rock is in Shelter Cove.

Right: Harbor Seals bask on Seal Rock in Shelter Cove. The rocks and islands scattered along the Humboldt coast are protected in the California Coastal National Monument. They provide important sheltering and breeding habitat for marine mammals and birds.

Little Black Sand Beach, on the north side of Shelter Cove, gives a view of the crumbling cliffs of the Lost Coast. Because these coastal mountains are extremely active seismically and are so sheer and erosive, early road builders sanely decided that a coastal highway through Humboldt County was not possible.

Humboldt Wild

Above: Backpackers trek on the Lost Coast Beach. A large portion of the route requires traversing rocks and soft sand; an awareness of high tides and wave size is essential for safe passage.

Right: Waves pounding Little Black Sand Beach show the fury of winter storms.

Left: The northern segment of the Lost Coast trail spans 25 miles of dramatic seascape. The King Range and its beaches constitute one of the largest designated Coastal Wilderness Areas in the Continental U.S.

Above: A rockfish head on an old fence post at Big Flat is a bit of earth art for the occasional passerby.

Humboldt Wild

Wild Cat Road, just north of Petrolia, parallels a small stretch
of vehicle-accessible beach and was one of the first highways
to be built in Humboldt County.

Southern

Left: A rainbow over Pratt Mountain lights up the dry meadows.

Right: An Oregon oak (*Quercus garryana*) displays its fall colors at sunset.

Left: Autumn raindrops, from the reflected oak trees above, are a welcome shift from the hot dry summer.

Above: A Pileated Woodpecker eyes the opportunity for insects in the bark of an Oregon oak.

Humboldt Wild

Fall meets winter in a mixed oak and Douglas-fir woodland on a high inland hill in southern Humboldt.

Left: A winter view from Bell Springs Road, looking east toward the Yola Bolly Wilderness and Black Rock Mountain.

Above: Snow depths vary dramatically with elevation and occasionally drop down to sea level.

  Humboldt Wild

Southern Humboldt hills slumber in the snow making the
day look monochrome.

Central Humboldt

Above: Victorian Old Town, Eureka

Right: Aleutian Geese take flight at sunrise during their annual migration to Humboldt Bay National Wildlife Refuge.

Humboldt Wild

Left: Old Bridgeville bridge was built in 1925 over the Van Duzen River, a tributary of the Eel.

Above: Old Van Duzen Bridge, a few miles west of Bridgeville, was also built in 1925. Neither bridge is in use now, but they serve as reminders of days long gone.

Humboldt Wild

The Van Duzen River meanders through forestland, including groves of ancient redwoods accessible by Highway 36.

An aerial view of Hydesville, its farms, airstrip and the braided confluence of the Van Duzen River as it flows into the main stem of the Eel River.

  Humboldt Wild

Looking down on the bridges spanning the Eel River and connecting Pacific Lumber company towns of Rio Dell and Scotia. The newer bridge is Highway 101, the smaller bridge called Eagle Prairie, was built in the 1940's. Scotia was established in 1863 and is now undergoing changes as the mills close.

Left: The Riverwalk in Fortuna tops Sandy Prairie levee, which stretches along the east bank of the Eel River.

Above: Domestically raised buffalo lounge outside a farmhouse in Fortuna.

Fortuna from above, backed by Redwood forests

Left: The Victorian-era town of Ferndale features a country museum with exhibits of antique clothing, furniture, farm machinery, and logging tools, as well as a blacksmith shop and an exhibit about the local dairy industry.

Above: Ferndale's cows have it pretty good in the Eel River floodplain.

 Humboldt Wild

Fernbridge was built over a lower reach of the Eel River in 1911 after the delta flooded and cut access to Ferndale. This Historical Landmark connects the lowland of Ferndale to Highway 101.

 Humboldt Wild

Left: The entire town of Ferndale, with its quaint Victorian architecture, has been designated a State Historical Landmark.

Above: The Black-crowned Night Heron is among the region's winged residents common year round.

A bench under a redwood tree beckons passersby to pause
next to Zipporah Pond in Ferndale's Russ Park, walking
distance from town center.

Left: The 2,200-acre Humboldt Bay National Wildlife Refuge is a mosaic-patterned estuary of varying depths, rich in salt marsh vegetation including Eelgrass, Salt grass, Cord grass and Pickle-weed. It is a nursery and habitat for many species such as Rockfish, Leopard Shark, Bay Pipe-fish, Salmon, and Steelhead.

Above: Brown Pelicans on Klopp Lake in the Arcata Marsh

Right: Willet in winter plumage

North winds make for good parasailing across the South Spit, which divides the Pacific Ocean and Humboldt Bay in Eureka.

Humboldt Wild

Humboldt Bay's South Spit has six miles of beach under restoration by the BLM. Ice plant and Yellow Lupine are exotic species imported from central California at one time to help stabilize the dunes, but unfortunately they have edged out native dune species.

Stretching for 34 miles along the Pacific coast, Humboldt Bay's beaches and sand dunes comprise the largest continuous dune system in northern California. This unique and vulnerable area hosts a variety of wildlife, including the endangered Western Snowy Plover.

Humboldt Wild

Above: Which ever way you chose to climb a sand dune, it's still slow going.

Right: Dune formation is a dynamic process requiring a source of sand, a shoreline perpendicular to prevailing winds, a low landscape over which sand can migrate and plant species adapted to survive drying winds and shifting ground. In Humboldt, the Eel and Mad Rivers supply most of the sand by winter flooding. It is then carried by currents along the coast and pushed up on beaches. Once dry, the sand is moved from the northwest by summer winds.

Left: The town of Samoa was built for workers at the large pulp mill nearby.

Above: Great Blue Heron—Industry and wildlife co-mingle in the Humboldt Bay.

 Humboldt Wild

Table Bluff Lighthouse, erected in 1892, four miles south of
the entrance to Humboldt Bay; it was deactivated in 1975
and then moved to Woodley Island near Eureka in 1987.

Aerial view of Eureka, Humboldt's county seat

Humboldt Wild

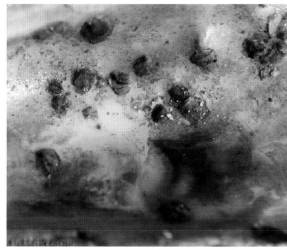

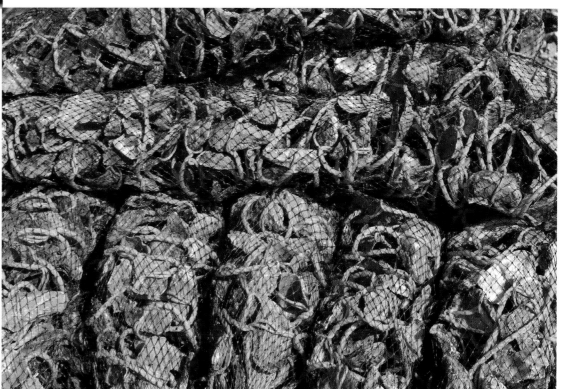

Above: An average of 18 months passes from "seed" oyster to harvest. The oyster larvae attaches to a fully mature shell that has been recycled. The brown spots are the new shells of the baby oysters.

Right: More than 70% of fresh oysters consumed in California are aqua-farmed in 450 acres of Arcata Bay. The "seeded" oysters are tethered to posts in the water and no harmful dredging is necessary to harvest them.

A redwood clearcut in Headwaters Forest east of Fortuna amidst second-growth and old-growth trees, photographed in 1995. Four years later, as a result of many years of environmental activism on the behalf of the unlogged ancient redwoods, the federal and California State government purchased 7,500 acres of Headwaters Forest from Pacific Lumber Company to create the publicly owned Headwaters Forest Reserve.

Humboldt Wild

Quoth the Raven, "Nevermore." Environmentalists favor
sustainable, low impact tree harvesting over clearcutting.

The 307-acre Arcata Marsh is a wildlife sanctuary as well as wastewater treatment system. This innovative restoration effort is internationally recognized for its use of marsh to treat the city of Arcata's wastewater in controlled stages of natural decomposition. The nutrient-rich habitat attracts thousands of birds representing 270-plus species. The light green vegetation, Duckweed, is a naturally occurring food source for many ducks.

Humboldt Wild

Above: Great Blue Heron

Center: Marbled Godwit and Short-billed Dowitcher

Right: Great Egret fishes at the mouth of Butcher's Slough.

Left: This spruce tree straddles an ancient redwood stump that became its "nurse log". The Arcata Community Forest includes old-growth redwoods, second-growth mixed forest and some massive stumps from logging that took place a century ago.

Above: The 620-acre Arcata Community Forest was dedicated in 1955. Located behind Humboldt State University, it includes 10 miles of roads and trails.

 Humboldt Wild

Above and Right: Azalea State Reserve in McKinleyville includes 30 acres of native Western Azaleas that bloom from April to May.

Mill Creek Falls in McKinleyville

Humboldt Wild

The Mad River empties into the Pacific at McKinleyville. Between town and the river runs
the Hammond Trail, popular for hiking and biking.

Autumn in the Six Rivers National Forest from Brush Mountain
east of Willow Creek

A favorite spot for summer swimming and boating, the
Trinity River flows through Six Rivers National Forest near
Willow Creek.

Northern Humboldt

Above: Mountain lions roam the wilds throughout Humboldt.

Right: The confluence of the mighty Klamath and Trinity rivers is at Weitchpec in northern Humboldt County. The Yurok Indian Reservation extends from here to the ocean for a mile on either side of the Klamath River. The Hoopa Valley Indian Reservation extends south along the Trinity River to a point north of Willow Creek. The Klamath is more nutrient rich due to marsh tannins up-river which cause it to be browner than the Trinity.

Humboldt Wild

Part of the Trinity Alps Wilderness extends into the eastern portion of Humboldt County.

A grove of Big-leaf maples in autumn lights up an old-growth
Douglas-fir forest.

Traditional Hoopa homes, called Xhontas, along the Trinity River

Humboldt Wild

The Hoopa Valley Indian Reservation straddles the Trinity River.

The Klamath River

Humboldt Wild

Jutting into the Pacific, Trinidad Head is an enormous chunk of volcanic rock left here when the Pacific plate dove beneath the North American plate 60 to 120 million years ago. Waves deposit sand in the lee of the rock, building up a spit that connects it with the mainland, Trinidad.

The only working lighthouse in Humboldt County today, Trinidad Lighthouse has been in continuous operation since 1871.

Above: Both the gull and the boats moored at Trinidad Bay seem to be taking some time off work on this overcast day.

Right: Trinidad Bay, looking south—These sea stacks are protected within the California Coastal National Monument.

The sun sets behind Trinidad Head for a perfect day's end.

The moon sets behind Pewetole Island, between Trinidad
State Park and College Cove.

Left: South toward Little River and Clam Beach, between Trinidad and McKinleyville, pounding ocean waves and coastal streams erode bluffs and build beaches.

Above: Waves at Patrick's Point north of Trinidad—Harder, more resistant rock, such as basalt and greenstone, withstand the erosive force to become steep headlands.

Humboldt Wild

Agate Beach is situated between Patrick's Point and Big Lagoon.

Left: Yurok sweathouses were built mostly underground with a separate entrance and exit. They were used for bathing and ritual purification by men and sometimes by the medicine women.

Above: A Yurok Sumeg Village with structures like this dwelling made of redwood planks can still be seen in Patrick's Point State Park. The ancestral villages of the Yurok spanned the coastal region from Trinidad Head to Beach Creek, and several miles upstream along the Klamath River.

Humboldt Wild

Looking south, Humboldt Lagoons State Park includes Big
Lagoon at the top, the small Dry Lagoon wedged between
Big Lagoon and Stone Lagoon, with Freshwater Lagoon at
the bottom. These are important resting and feeding sites
for thousands of birds during winter migration along the
Pacific Flyway.

Left: Largest of the region's coastal lagoons, Big Lagoon is breached several times each winter by ocean waves.

Above: Sitka spruce cluster on the edge of Big Lagoon. Humboldt County is the southern reach of this Pacific Northwest conifer species.

Right: Sailboats beached at Big Lagoon

Backed by forested slopes and fronted by driftwood, Dry Lagoon is actually a freshwater marsh that provides habitat for ducks, bitterns, and herons.

Humboldt Wild

The beach at Dry Lagoon looking north toward Sharp Point

Left: Beach Silvertop (*Glehnia littoralis*) at Stone Lagoon

Above: When Stone Lagoon's sand spit is breached by winter storms anadromous fish (salmon and steelhead) enter from the sea.

  Humboldt Wild

Lupines bloom in the foreground of mile-long Freshwater Lagoon, home to waterfowl, mink, river otter, and stocked trout.

Left: During rutting season, bull Roosevelt elk are especially dangerous as they spar for mates.

Above: Though Prairie Creek Redwoods State Park is home to the largest herd of Roosevelt elk, they often wander to graze the grounds of the Red Schoolhouse in nearby Orick.

Humboldt Wild

Gold Bluffs Beach is both golden in color and a historic
source of true gold dust.

Sunlight streams through some of the world's tallest trees in Lady Bird Johnson Grove in Redwood National and State Park.

Humboldt Wild

The majestic redwoods at Lady Bird Johnson Grove tower over hikers.

Humboldt Wild

Left: Leather fern (*Polypodium scouleri*) growing on a Sitka spruce—These ferns seldom grow in soil, but prefer to grow on tree bark in moist coastal forests.

Top: Delicate new growth on the tips of a Sitka spruce

Above: Young male cones of a Sitka spruce

Above: Fern Canyon was carved by Home Creek through sedimentary soil over the eons. Its 50-80-foot walls host eight species of ferns and other moisture loving plants and mosses.

Right: Five-fingered ferns (*Adiantum pedatum*) are most abundant in Fern Canyon.

Special Events

Above: Having fun at the Festival of Courage in Blue Lake

Right: The Clam Beach Run starts the year off with a 5.75 and an 8.75-mile run from Trinidad to Clam Beach in McKinleyville. The most challenging part is crossing Little River, swollen by winter rain, at Moonstone Beach. Coast Guards are nearby to help the runners of all ages.

Humboldt Wild

  Humboldt Wild

Left: The Redwood Region Logging Conference in March aims to educate the community about natural resource management using demonstrations, historical displays, competitive events, and a career day for students.

Above: Falk 1 on display at the logging conference. It was the first steam locomotive used by the Elk River Mill lumber company in 1885.

Above & Right: The Redwood Coast Jazz Festival in March features jazz, swing, calypso, zydeco, and more! A Big Band Dance at Eureka's Adorni Center kicks off the three-day festival.

Among many others, Dr. Seuss characters take "The Perilous Plunge" into the icy Humboldt Bay to raise funds for the Redwood Discovery Museum in Eureka.

Humboldt Wild

Above: A Northern Spotted Owl closes in on a mouse set as bait by naturalists monitoring this endangered species. This rare opportunity to observe the owls in their nesting habitat is offered during Godwit Days.

Right: Godwits feed during low tide. April's Godwit Days celebrates the spring migration of this native shorebird with a weeklong festival including nearly 100 field trips, lectures, and workshops with expert birders.

Humboldt Wild

Above: The springtime Rhododendron Parade in downtown Eureka celebrates the community's public safety heroes.

Right: The Tour of the Unknown Coast is a 100-mile bicycle race through some of Humboldt County's most beautiful and steepest terrain. Here bikers "hit the wall" above Sugarloaf Island near Cape Mendocino, a one-mile, 18%-grade incline.

The Kinetic Sculpture Race and Festival, founded by Hobart Brown in 1969, is a hilarious and unique event featuring human-powered all-terrain amphibious sculptures racing three days over a tortuous 42-mile course of sand, water, mud, and other obstacles. Celebrating art, invention, and endurance the Kinetic Sculpture Race is spirited fun!

Above & Right: Only the most durable contraptions and lucky competitors in the Kinetic Sculpture Race make it to the finish line. The course runs from Arcata to Ferndale and all sculptures must carry flotation devices to cross Humboldt Bay, the Eel River, and Morgan's Slough.

Left: The Redwood Run is an opportunity for Harley-Davidson owners and other bikers to listen to great music, talk bikes, and ride together on Humboldt County's scenic roads. Now in its fourth decade, the Redwood Run is an established summer tradition.

Above: The Redwood Run campsite is located in Piercy, a few miles south of the Humboldt County line in Mendocino County, but Garberville is the event's town base.

Above & Right: The popular Summer Arts and Music Festival at Benbow Lake State Recreation Area features five stages, over a hundred diverse performances, craft booths and kid zones. Dream catchers and belly dancing are among the intriguing offerings.

The outdoor venue at Benbow Lake State Recreation Area
is a great place for concerts such as Jazz on the Lake.

Humboldt Wild

The town of Garberville hosts a parade each year on
Rodeo Weekend. Here, an improvised steer snorts smoke.

The Sand Sculpture Contest in Manila requires that only materials found on the beach be used.

Humboldt Wild

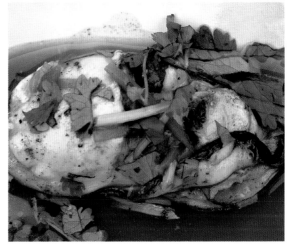

Above: The popular Oyster Festival takes place in June on the Arcata Plaza.

Right: Many restaurants compete for the best oyster recipe.

Humboldt Wild

Above: The Fish Festival in Trinidad is another opportunity to taste the fabulous fare from the sea and celebrate its abundance.

Right: An egret listens to the blues from Woodley Island during Blues on the Bay, a summer music festival that takes place on Humboldt Bay in Eureka.

Left, Center, and Above: For 86 years, cowboys and cowgirls from all over California have come to the Fortuna Rodeo, making it the oldest continuous rodeo on the North Coast.

Humboldt Wild

Above and Right: The annual Fortuna Redwood AutoXpo draws thousands of spectators for three days to view vintage cars, antique tractors, and farm equipment.

Left: The seven-day Dell' Arte Mad River Festival includes performances in theatre, music, comedy, storytelling, puppetry, and lots of folk music.

Above: The Annie and Mary Day Fiddle Festival kicks off the week long Humboldt Folklife Festival.

 Humboldt Wild

Above and Right: At Annie and Mary Day, the Dell'Arte theatre group leads an "allegory parade" where good overcomes evil.

Left: Michael Franti makes contact with the audience at Reggae on the River.

Above: Colorful performers take the stage at ROTR.

 Humboldt Wild

Above: A dreadlocked fan remembers Bob Marley, a pioneer of reggae music.

Right: Reggae on the River, a southern Humboldt festival, attracts thousands to the "Irie" vibes.

  Humboldt Wild

Above: Michael Muir, John Muir's great grandson, drives a wheelchair-accessible horse drawn carriage across Bear River in Capetown, near Cape Mendocino. His Access Adventure program provides wilderness and open-space access to people with disabilities.

Right: Reggae Riding Mountain Bike Fest is an inter-generational all day event at the Southern Humboldt Community Park.

Left: Since 1896, the annual Humboldt County Fair in Ferndale has been a county-wide celebration. It features exhibits, carnivals, live entertainment, livestock auctions, and livestock contests for 4H clubs.

Above: Though the Cape Mendocino Lighthouse is now in Shelter Cove, its original optic lens greets visitors at the entrance to the Humboldt County Fairgrounds.

Horse racing is old style fun at the Humboldt County Fair.

Left: "A Taste of the Cove" is an autumn salmon BBQ in Shelter Cove to benefit Heart of the Redwoods Hospice in Garberville.

Above: The "Flaming Chefs" serve up the tasty meal.

 Humboldt Wild

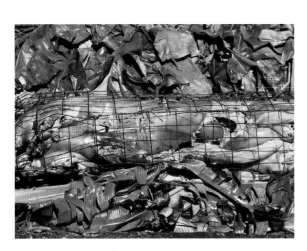

Above: Local radio station KMUD, "People-Powered Radio", hosts an annual Hawaiian-style Luai complete with roasted pig covered by banana and tea leaves slowly cooked in an earthen pit.

Right: Hawaiian music and Hula dancers entertain the audience.

Left: The "Wild Things" come to entertain and revel at the North County Fair.

Above and Right: The All Species Parade during the North County Fair in Arcata is a playful event honoring our animal friends.

Humboldt Wild

Left: Earth First! activist Judi Bari, holding a poster of Headwaters Forest, was a leader in the movement to protect the last remaining ancient redwoods.

Above: Rallies to save Headwaters Forest, finally protected in 1999, were an annual event for a few years. Singer-songwriter Bonnie Raitt (center) and Micky Hart of the Grateful Dead (right) join the protest.

Protecting the last ancient redwood trees from the chainsaw seems to be a perennial activity among Humboldt citizens and committed visitors. Julia "Butterfly" Hill was among the more high-profile activists, living in an old-growth redwood tree, named Luna, for two full years. Here she waves from the top of her perch.

Left: Leon Russell headlines the Woof Fest, a benefit for the Sequoia Humane Society in Eureka.

Above: Dogs of all breeds get to meet one another at the Woof Fest.

 Humboldt Wild

Above: Kayaking Days corresponds with the Maritime Expo and makes for a very busy Humboldt Bay as the Madaket vessel shuttles people to and from Woodley Island.

Right: The Maritime Expo at Woodley Island in Eureka celebrates the important work of the US Coast Guard.

Humboldt Wild

Left: A Taste of Willow Creek is an opportunity to tour farms and vineyards nestled in the heart of the Six Rivers National Forest.

Above: Relaxing at Winnett Vineyards.

Above: A sampling of local produce at Willow Creek Farms during Taste of Willow Creek

Right: Ornamental peppers grown in a green house at River Nook Orchard

Special Events

The Festival of Courage in Blue Lake recreates a medieval village with live jousting, Celtic music, and other remnants of an era long gone.

Humboldt Wild

Above: Kids duel at the Festival of Courage.

Right: This woman demonstrates the art of chain-mail armor fabrication.

Left: Humboldt Gay Pride Parade in Arcata

Above: A Sister of Perpetual Indulgence

Humboldt Wild

Pastels on the Plaza in Arcata

Left and Above: The Apple Harvest Festival in Fortuna includes the opportunity for a hayride to a local apple farm for fresh cider.

An auction during Fortuna's Apple Harvest Festival mirrors the old and the new communities.

The Humboldt Redwoods Marathon and Half-Marathon takes place in the shady depths of Humboldt Redwoods State Park.

Above: The Fall Farm Tour in Central Humboldt is an opportunity to visit local farms and purchase their harvests.

Right: A corn maize at Potter's Produce in Blue Lake entertains the kids.

Arcata
707-822-3619
www.arcatachamber.com

Blue Lake
707-668-5567
www.bluelakechamber.com

Eureka
707-442-3738
www.eurekachamber.com

Ferndale
707-786-4477
www.victorianferndale.org/chamber

Fortuna
707-725-3959
www.chamber.sunnyfortuna.com

Garberville-Redway
800-923-2613
www.garberville.org

McKinleyville
707-839-2449
www.mckinleyvillechamber.com

Orick
707-488-2885
www.orick.net

Rio Dell
707-764-3436
www.riodellscotiachamber.org

Trinidad
707-677-1610
www.discovertrinidadca.com

Willow Creek
530-629-2693
www.willowcreekchamber.com

**Humboldt County Convention
& Visitors Bureau**
707-443-5097
www.redwoodvisitor.org